HAL•LEONARD

JAZZ PLAY-ALONG®

Book & Audio for B♭, E♭, C and Bass Clef Instruments

volume 91

Produced by Don Sickler

THELONIOUS MONK FAVORITES

T0045405

PLAYBACK+
Speed • Pitch • Balance • Loop

To access audio, visit:
www.halleonard.com/mylibrary

1196-5262-4117-4539

Cover photo: © Michael Ochs Archive / Getty Images

ISBN 978-0-7935-8761-2

HAL•LEONARD®

For all works contained herein:
Unauthorized copying, arranging, adapting, recording, internet posting, public performance,
or other distribution of the music in this publication is an infringement of copyright.
Infringers are liable under the law.

Visit Hal Leonard Online at
www.halleonard.com

World headquarters, contact:
Hal Leonard
7777 West Bluemound Road
Milwaukee, WI 53213
Email: info@halleonard.com

In Europe, contact:
Hal Leonard Europe Limited
1 Red Place
London, W1K 6PL
Email: info@halleonardeurope.com

In Australia, contact:
Hal Leonard Australia Pty. Ltd.
4 Lentara Court
Cheltenham, Victoria, 3192 Australia
Email: info@halleonard.com.au

Thelonious Monk Favorites

Volume 91

Produced by
Don Sickler

Featured Players:

Don Sickler–Trumpet
Ronnie Mathews–Piano
Kiyoshi Kitagawa–Bass
Ben Riley–Drums

**Recorded, mixed, and mastered by Rudy Van Gelder,
Van Gelder Recording Studio, Inc.**

HOW TO USE THE AUDIO:

Each song has <u>two</u> tracks:

1) Split Track/Demonstration

Woodwind, Brass, Keyboard, and **Mallet Players** can use
this track as a learning tool for melody style and inflection.

Bass Players can learn and perform with this track –
remove the recorded bass track by turning down the
volume on the LEFT channel.

Keyboard and **Guitar Players** can learn and perform with
this track – remove the recorded piano part by turning down
the volume on the RIGHT channel.

2) Backing Track

Soloists or **Groups** can learn and perform with this
accompaniment track with the RHYTHM SECTION only.

LET'S CALL THIS

BY THELONIOUS MONK

C VERSION

(FINE ON D.S.)

Copyright © 1978 by Thelonious Music Corp.
This arrangement Copyright © 2010 by Thelonious Music Corp.
International Copyright Secured   All Rights Reserved

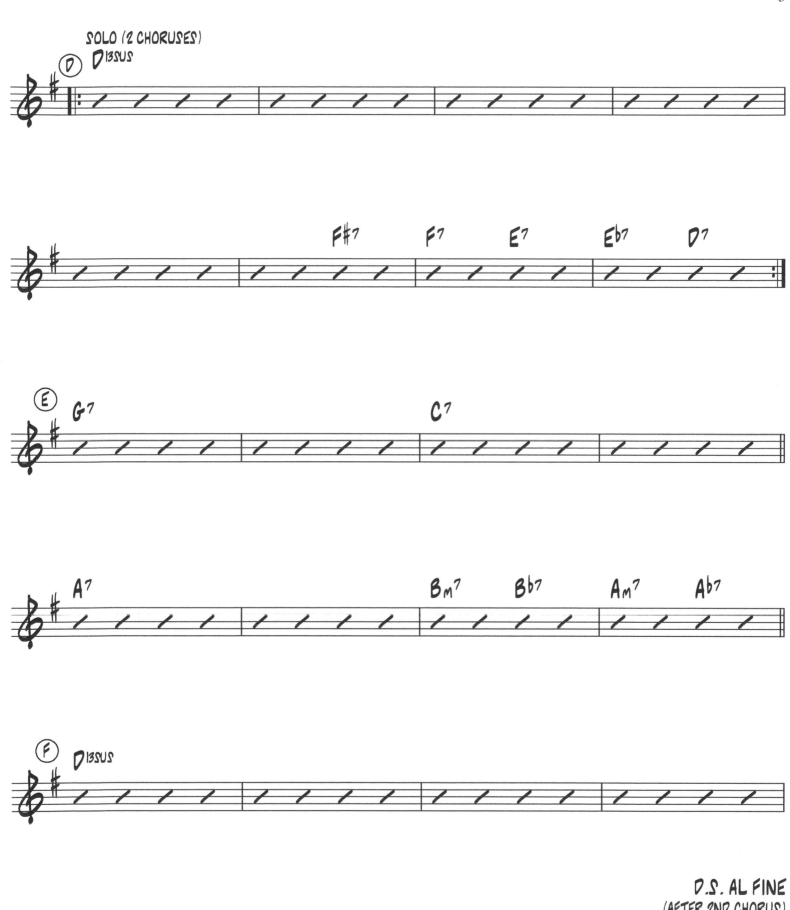

SOLO (2 CHORUSES)

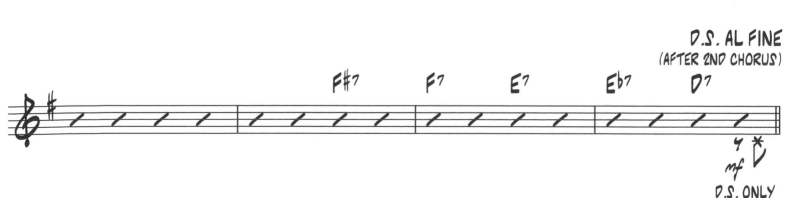

D.S. AL FINE
(AFTER 2ND CHORUS)

D.S. ONLY

PANNONICA

BY THELONIOUS MONK

C VERSION

Copyright © 1958 (Renewed 1986) by Thelonious Music Corp.
This arrangement Copyright © 2010 by Thelonious Music Corp.
International Copyright Secured   All Rights Reserved

D.S. AL FINE

BRIGHT MISSISSIPPI

C VERSION

BY THELONIOUS MONK

Copyright © 1978 by Thelonious Music Corp.
This arrangement Copyright © 2010 by Thelonious Music Corp.
International Copyright Secured   All Rights Reserved

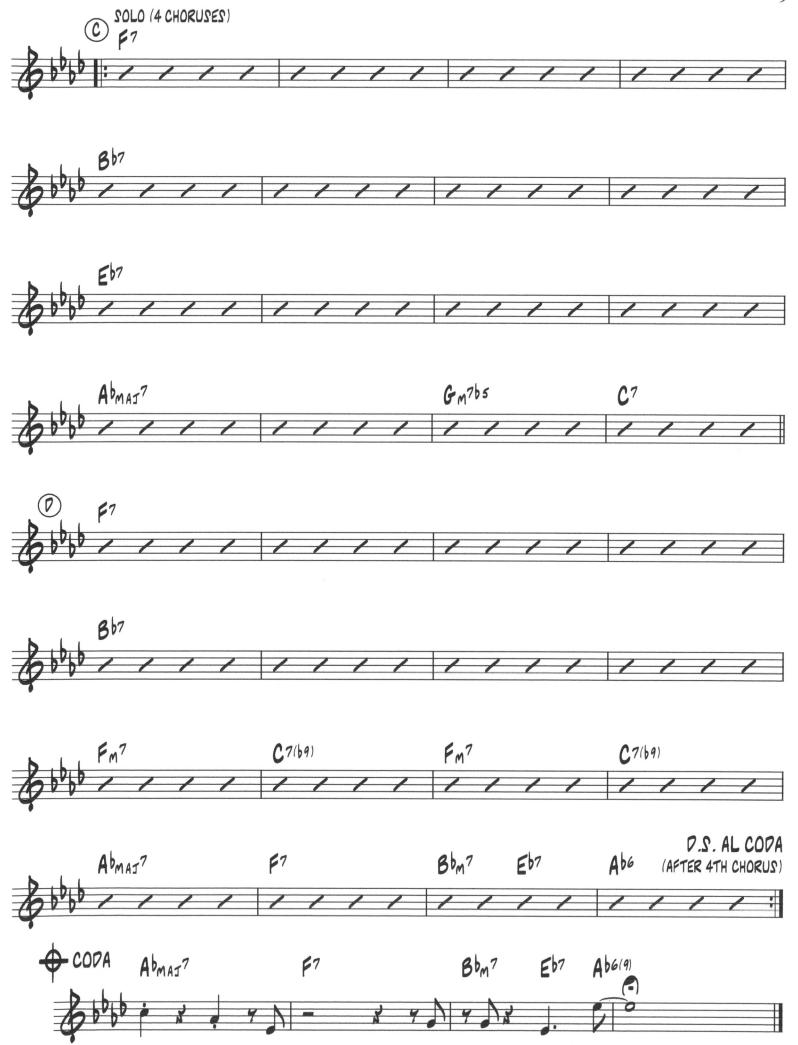

BEMSHA SWING

BY THELONIOUS MONK
AND DENZIL BEST

C VERSION

Copyright © 1952 (Renewed 1980) Second Floor Music
This arrangement Copyright © 2010 Second Floor Music
International Copyright Secured   All Rights Reserved

BLUE MONK

C VERSION

BY THELONIOUS MONK

Copyright © 1962 (Renewed 1990) by Thelonious Music Corp.
This arrangement Copyright © 2010 by Thelonious Music Corp.
International Copyright Secured   All Rights Reserved

'Round Midnight

MUSIC BY THELONIOUS MONK AND COOTIE WILLIAMS
WORDS BY BERNIE HANIGHEN

C VERSION

Copyright © 1944 (Renewed 1971) by Thelonious Music Corp. and Warner Bros. Inc.
This arrangement Copyright © 2010 by Thelonious Music Corp. and Warner Bros. Inc.
International Copyright Secured   All Rights Reserved

13

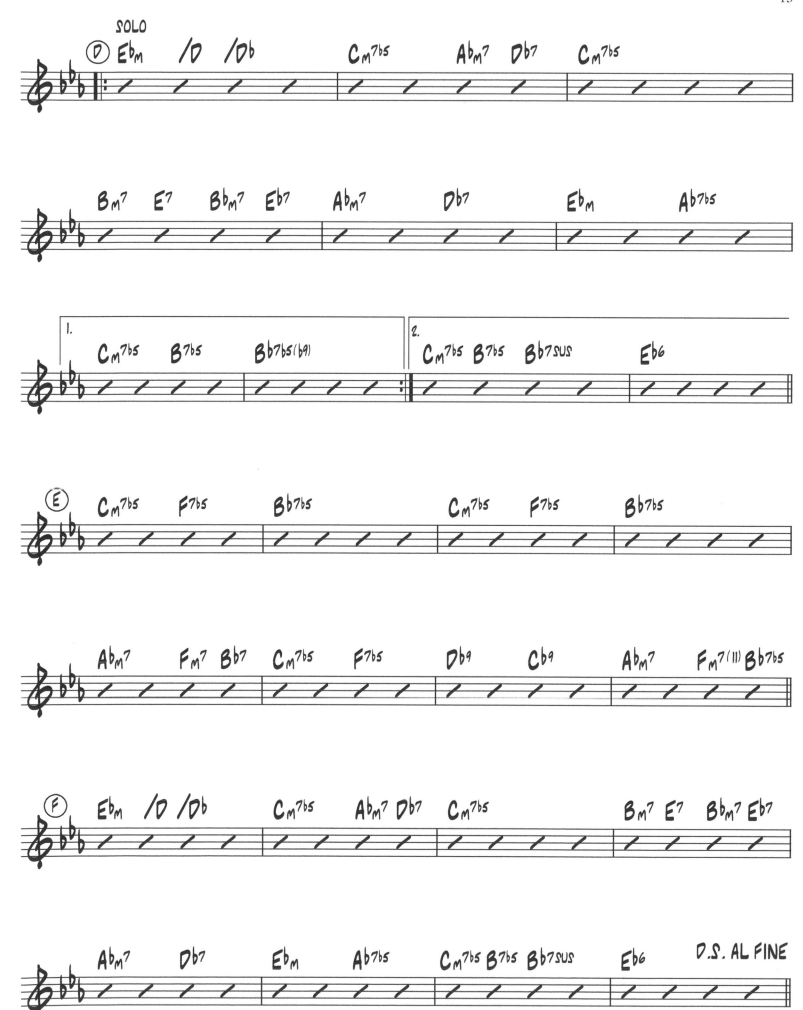

SHUFFLE BOIL

BY THELONIOUS MONK

C VERSION

Copyright © 1955 (Renewed 1984) by Thelonious Music Corp.
This arrangement Copyright © 2010 by Thelonious Music Corp.
International Copyright Secured   All Rights Reserved

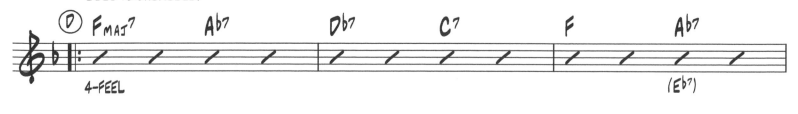

SOLO (2 CHORUSES)

4-FEEL

D.S. AL FINE
(AFTER 2ND CHORUS)

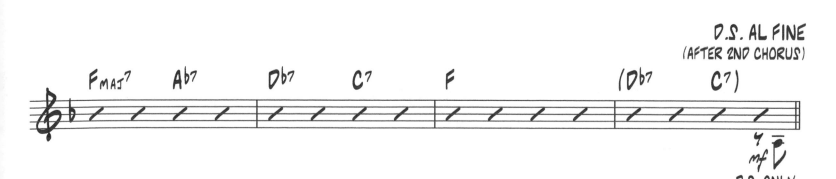

D.S. ONLY

UGLY BEAUTY

BY THELONIOUS MONK

C VERSION

* BOTH THE ♮5 AND ♭5 ARE VOICED IN THE HARMONY: THE ♮5 ABOVE THE ROOT, BELOW THE ♭5.

Copyright © 1978 by Thelonious Music Corp.
This arrangement Copyright © 2010 by Thelonious Music Corp.
International Copyright Secured   All Rights Reserved

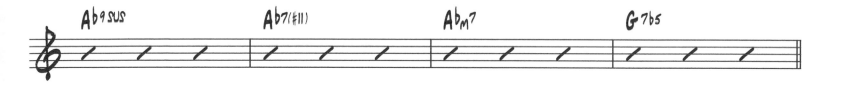

RHYTHM-A-NING

BY THELONIOUS MONK

C VERSION

Copyright © 1958 (Renewed 1986) by Thelonious Music Corp.
This arrangement Copyright © 2010 by Thelonious Music Corp.
International Copyright Secured   All Rights Reserved

BYE-YA

BY THELONIOUS MONK

C VERSION

(FINE ON D.S.)

Copyright © 1962 (Renewed 1990) by Thelonious Music Corp.
This arrangement Copyright © 2010 by Thelonious Music Corp.
International Copyright Secured   All Rights Reserved

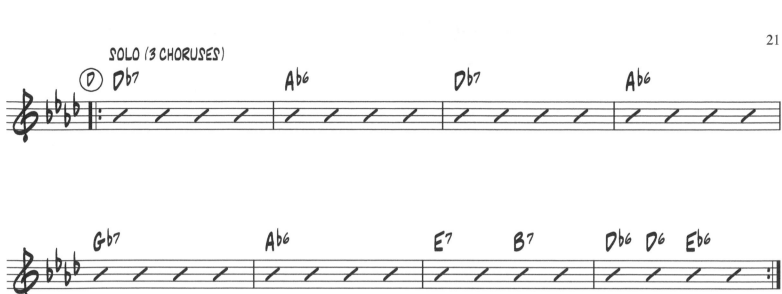

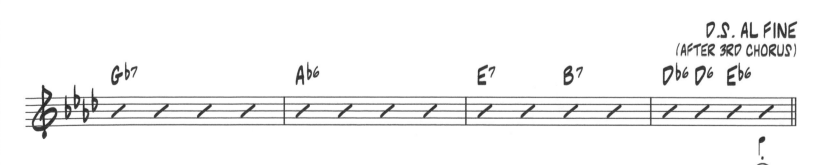

LET'S CALL THIS

BY THELONIOUS MONK

Bb VERSION

(FINE ON D.S.)

Copyright © 1978 by Thelonious Music Corp.
This arrangement Copyright © 2010 by Thelonious Music Corp.
International Copyright Secured   All Rights Reserved

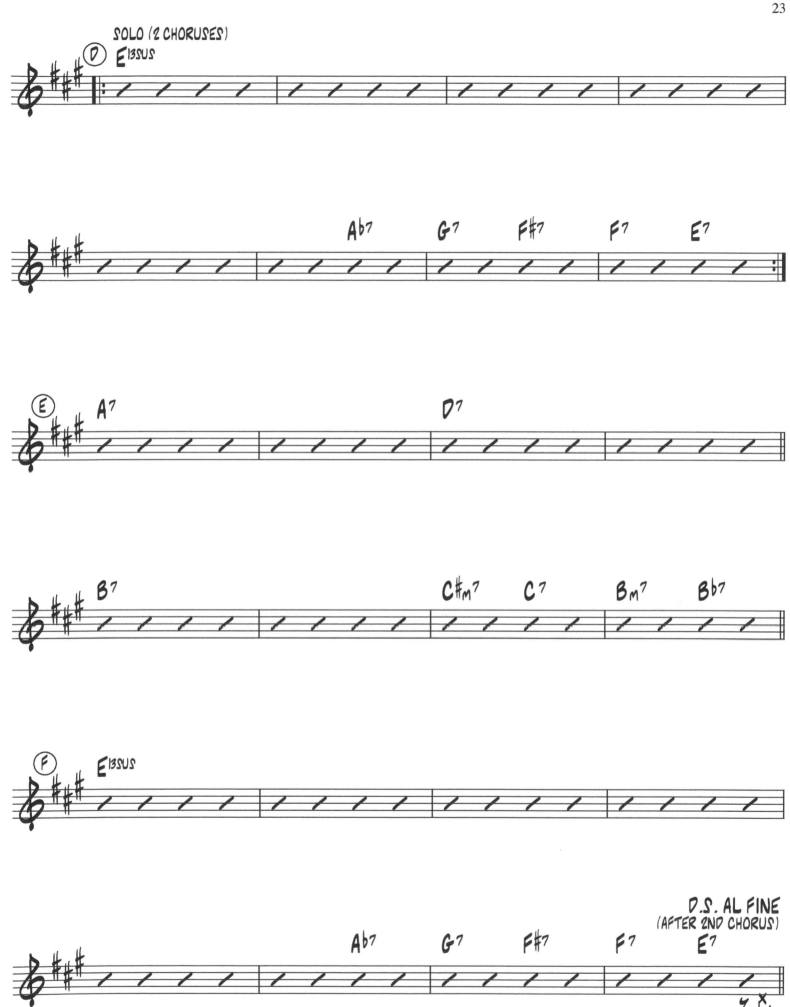

PANNONICA

BY THELONIOUS MONK

Copyright © 1958 (Renewed 1986) by Thelonious Music Corp.
This arrangement Copyright © 2010 by Thelonious Music Corp.
International Copyright Secured   All Rights Reserved

BRIGHT MISSISSIPPI

BY THELONIOUS MONK

Bb VERSION

Copyright © 1978 by Thelonious Music Corp.
This arrangement Copyright © 2010 by Thelonious Music Corp.
International Copyright Secured   All Rights Reserved

Bemsha Swing

BY THELONIOUS MONK
AND DENZIL BEST

Copyright © 1952 (Renewed 1980) Second Floor Music
This arrangement Copyright © 2010 Second Floor Music
International Copyright Secured   All Rights Reserved

BLUE MONK

BY THELONIOUS MONK

Bb VERSION

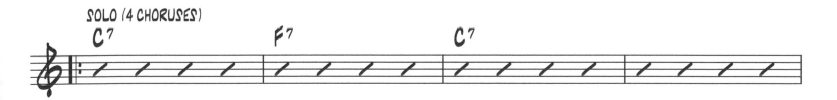

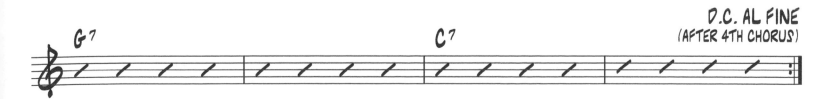

Copyright © 1962 (Renewed 1990) by Thelonious Music Corp.
This arrangement Copyright © 2010 by Thelonious Music Corp.
International Copyright Secured   All Rights Reserved

'Round Midnight

MUSIC BY THELONIOUS MONK AND COOTIE WILLIAMS
WORDS BY BERNIE HANIGHEN

Bb VERSION

Copyright © 1944 (Renewed 1971) by Thelonious Music Corp. and Warner Bros. Inc.
This arrangement Copyright © 2010 by Thelonious Music Corp. and Warner Bros. Inc.
International Copyright Secured   All Rights Reserved

SHUFFLE BOIL

BY THELONIOUS MONK

Copyright © 1955 (Renewed 1984) by Thelonious Music Corp.
This arrangement Copyright © 2010 by Thelonious Music Corp.
International Copyright Secured   All Rights Reserved

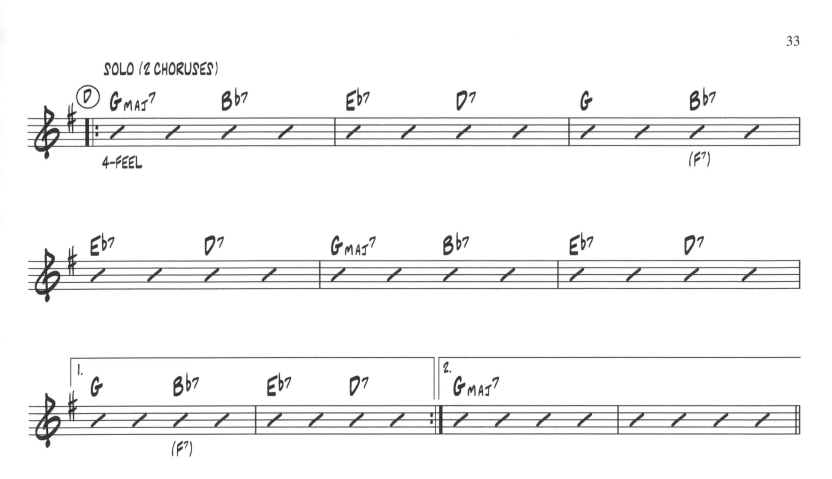

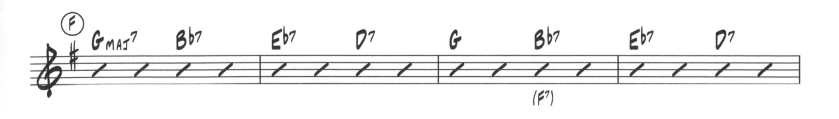

UGLY BEAUTY

BY THELONIOUS MONK

Bb VERSION

* BOTH THE ♮5 AND ♭5 ARE VOICED IN THE HARMONY: THE ♮5 ABOVE THE ROOT, BELOW THE ♭5.

Copyright © 1978 by Thelonious Music Corp.
This arrangement Copyright © 2010 by Thelonious Music Corp.
International Copyright Secured   All Rights Reserved

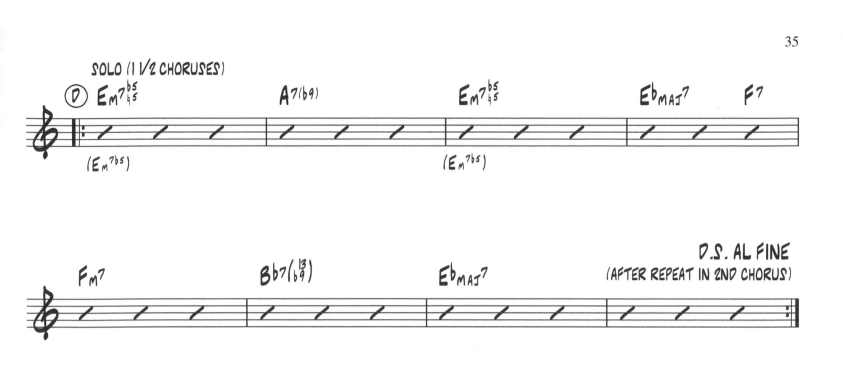

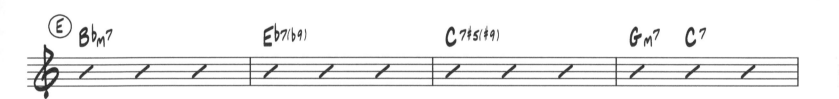

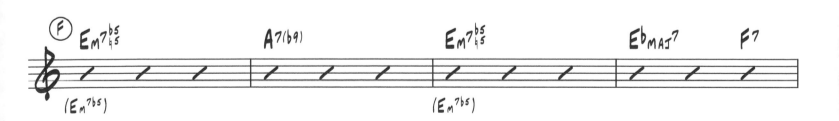

RHYTHM-A-NING

BY THELONIOUS MONK

Bb VERSION

MEDIUM SWING

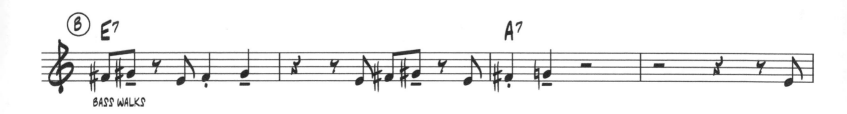

Copyright © 1958 (Renewed 1986) by Thelonious Music Corp.
This arrangement Copyright © 2010 by Thelonious Music Corp.
International Copyright Secured   All Rights Reserved

BYE-YA

BY THELONIOUS MONK

Bb VERSION

MEDIUM SWING

(FINE ON D.S.)

Copyright © 1962 (Renewed 1990) by Thelonious Music Corp.
This arrangement Copyright © 2010 by Thelonious Music Corp.
International Copyright Secured All Rights Reserved

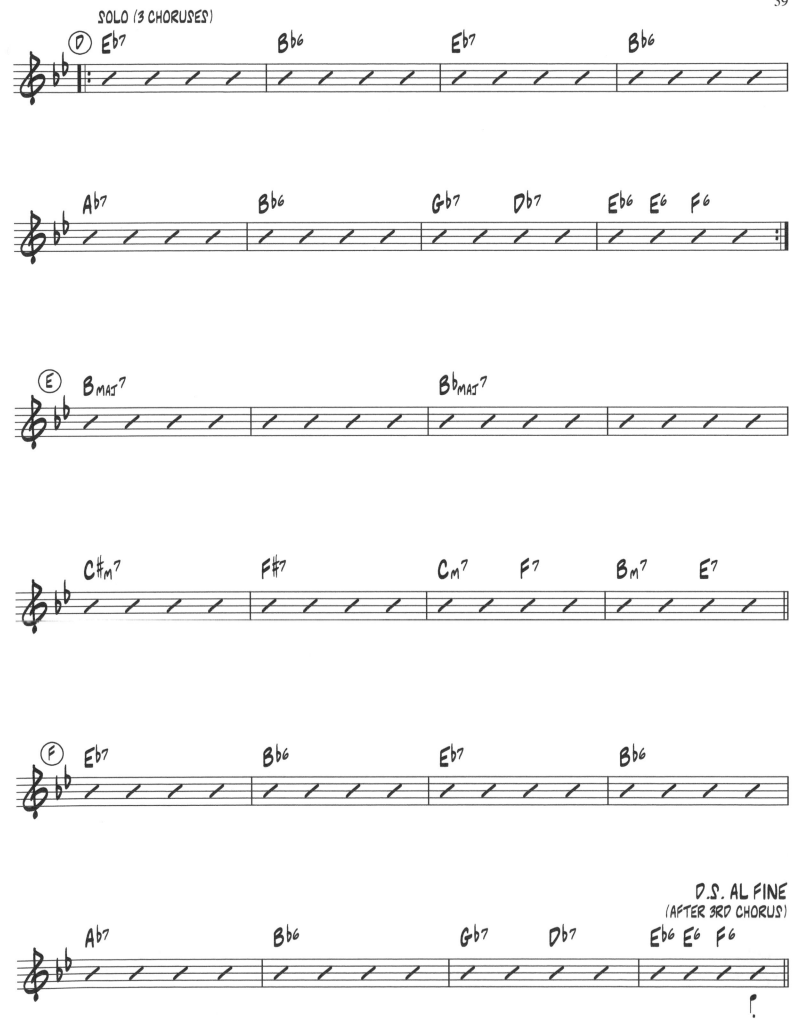

LET'S CALL THIS

BY THELONIOUS MONK

Copyright © 1978 by Thelonious Music Corp.
This arrangement Copyright © 2010 by Thelonious Music Corp.
International Copyright Secured   All Rights Reserved

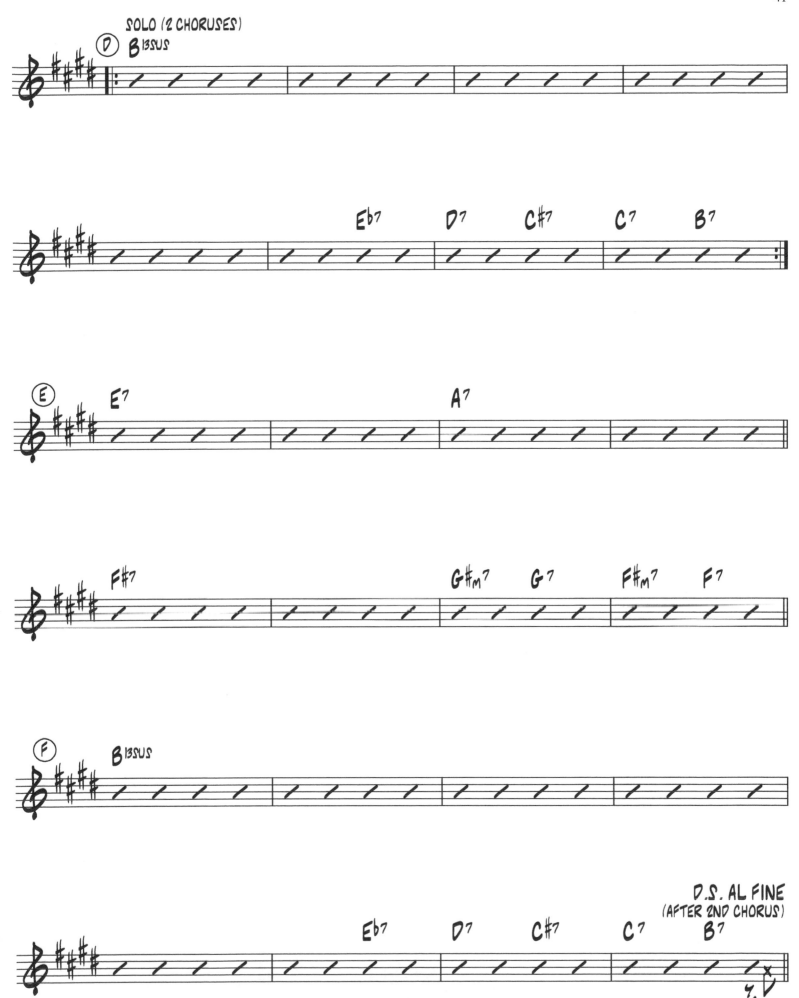

PANNONICA

BY THELONIOUS MONK

Copyright © 1958 (Renewed 1986) by Thelonious Music Corp.
This arrangement Copyright © 2010 by Thelonious Music Corp.
International Copyright Secured   All Rights Reserved

43

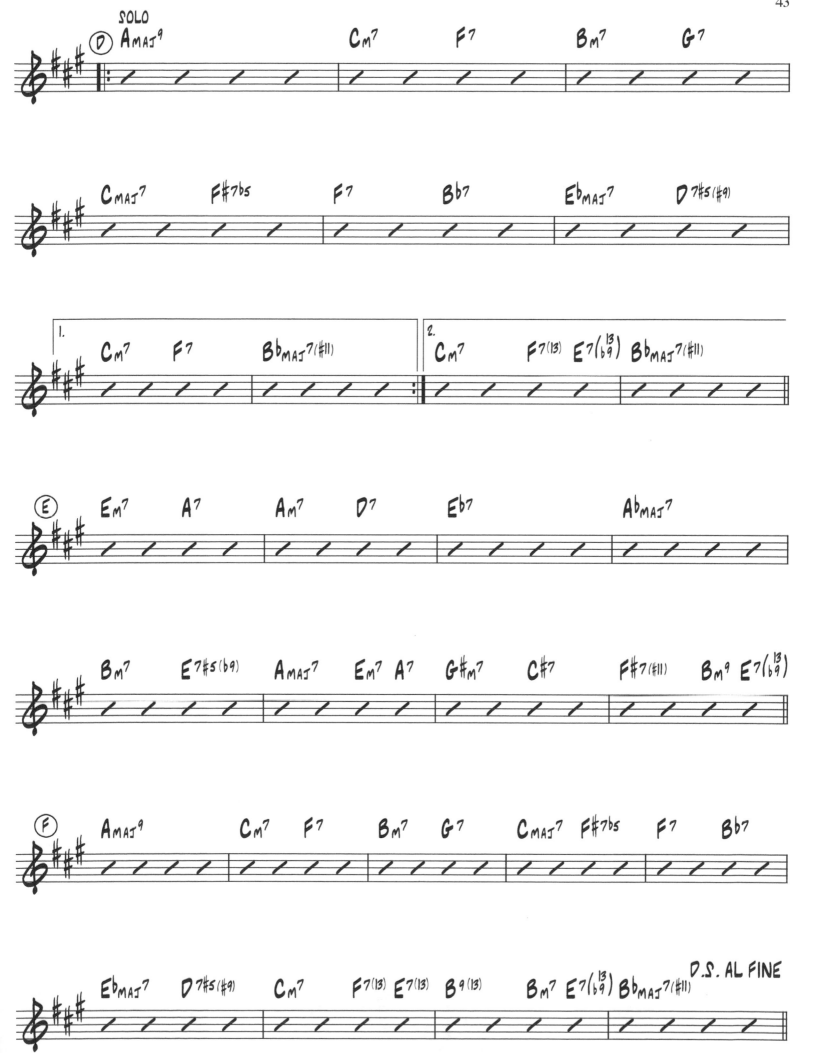

BRIGHT MISSISSIPPI

BY THELONIOUS MONK

Copyright © 1978 by Thelonious Music Corp.
This arrangement Copyright © 2010 by Thelonious Music Corp.
International Copyright Secured   All Rights Reserved

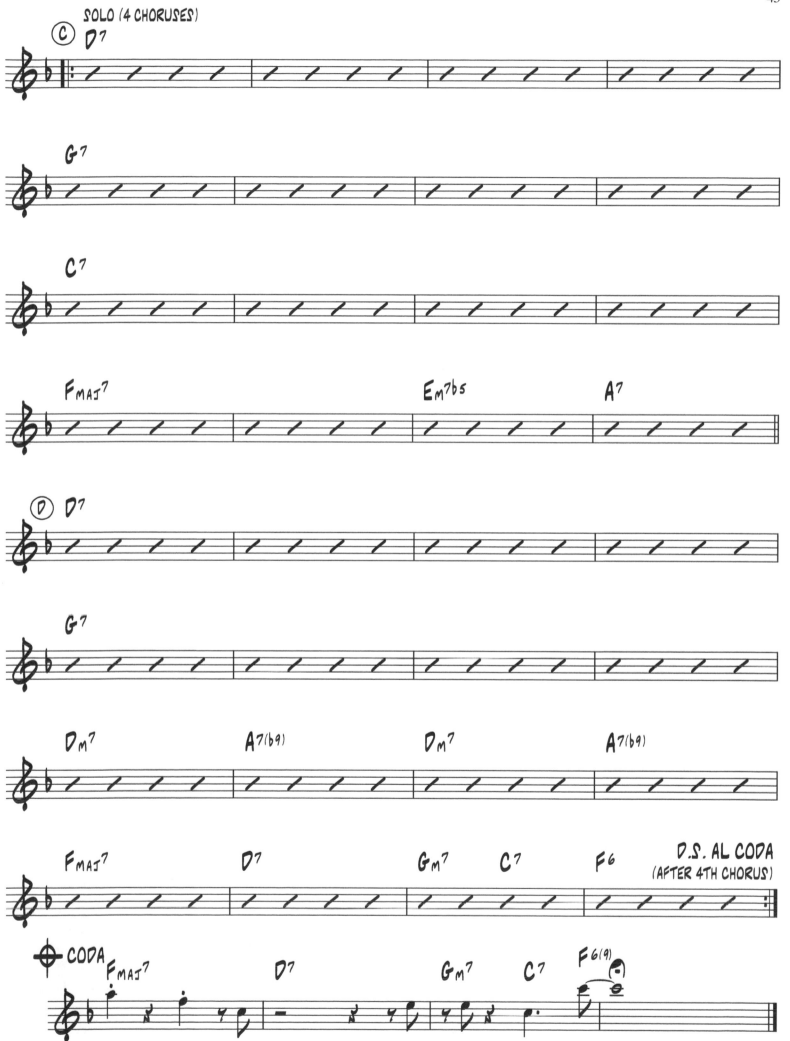

BEMSHA SWING

BY THELONIOUS MONK
AND DENZIL BEST

Copyright © 1952 (Renewed 1980) Second Floor Music
This arrangement Copyright © 2010 Second Floor Music
International Copyright Secured   All Rights Reserved

BLUE MONK

BY THELONIOUS MONK

Eb VERSION

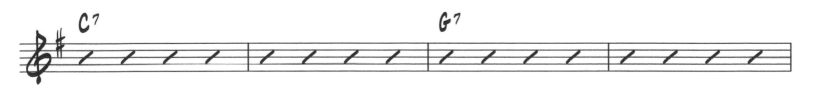

Copyright © 1962 (Renewed 1990) by Thelonious Music Corp.
This arrangement Copyright © 2010 by Thelonious Music Corp.
International Copyright Secured   All Rights Reserved

'Round Midnight

MUSIC BY THELONIOUS MONK AND COOTIE WILLIAMS
WORDS BY BERNIE HANIGHEN

Copyright © 1944 (Renewed 1971) by Thelonious Music Corp. and Warner Bros. Inc.
This arrangement Copyright © 2010 by Thelonious Music Corp. and Warner Bros. Inc.
International Copyright Secured   All Rights Reserved

SHUFFLE BOIL

BY THELONIOUS MONK

Copyright © 1955 (Renewed 1984) by Thelonious Music Corp.
This arrangement Copyright © 2010 by Thelonious Music Corp.
International Copyright Secured   All Rights Reserved

SOLO (2 CHORUSES)

ⓓ Dmaj7 | F7 | Bb7 | A7 | D | F7 (C7)

4-FEEL

Bb7 | A7 | Dmaj7 | F7 | Bb7 | A7

1. D | F7 (C7) | Bb7 | A7 : 2. Dmaj7 |

ⓔ Am7 | D7 | G7 | F#7

Bm7 | E7 | Em7 | A7

ⓕ Dmaj7 | F7 | Bb7 | A7 | D | F7 (C7) | Bb7 | A7

D.S. AL FINE
(AFTER 2ND CHORUS)

Dmaj7 | F7 | Bb7 | A7 | D | (Bb7 | A7)

mf

D.S. ONLY

UGLY BEAUTY

BY THELONIOUS MONK

Eb VERSION

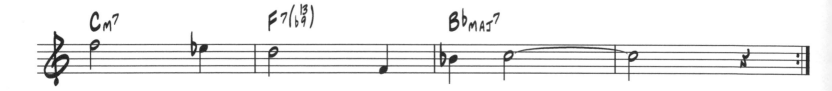

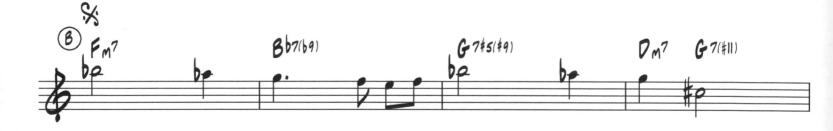

RIT. LAST TIME

* BOTH THE ♮5 AND ♭5 ARE VOICED IN THE HARMONY: THE ♮5 ABOVE THE ROOT, BELOW THE ♭5.

Copyright © 1978 by Thelonious Music Corp.
This arrangement Copyright © 2010 by Thelonious Music Corp.
International Copyright Secured   All Rights Reserved

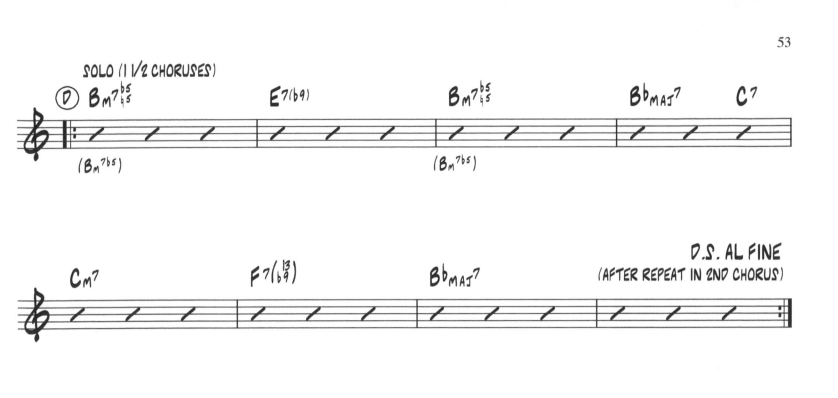

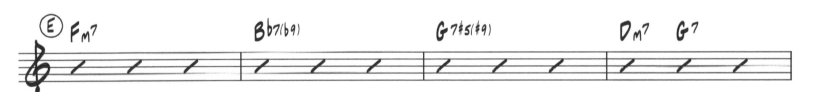

RHYTHM-A-NING

BY THELONIOUS MONK

Eb VERSION

Copyright © 1958 (Renewed 1986) by Thelonious Music Corp.
This arrangement Copyright © 2010 by Thelonious Music Corp.
International Copyright Secured   All Rights Reserved

BYE-YA

BY THELONIOUS MONK

Eb VERSION

(FINE ON D.S.)

Copyright © 1962 (Renewed 1990) by Thelonious Music Corp.
This arrangement Copyright © 2010 by Thelonious Music Corp.
International Copyright Secured   All Rights Reserved

Let's Call This

BY THELONIOUS MONK

𝄢: C VERSION

(FINE ON D.S.)

Copyright © 1978 by Thelonious Music Corp.
This arrangement Copyright © 2010 by Thelonious Music Corp.
International Copyright Secured   All Rights Reserved

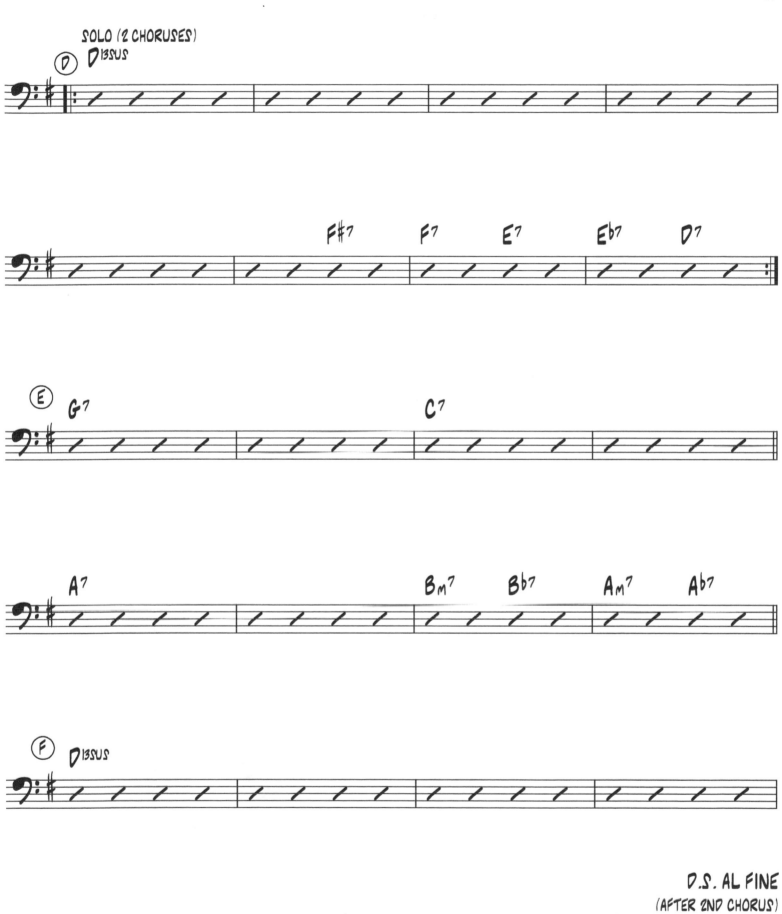

PANNONICA

𝄢 C VERSION

BY THELONIOUS MONK

Copyright © 1958 (Renewed 1986) by Thelonious Music Corp.
This arrangement Copyright © 2010 by Thelonious Music Corp.
International Copyright Secured   All Rights Reserved

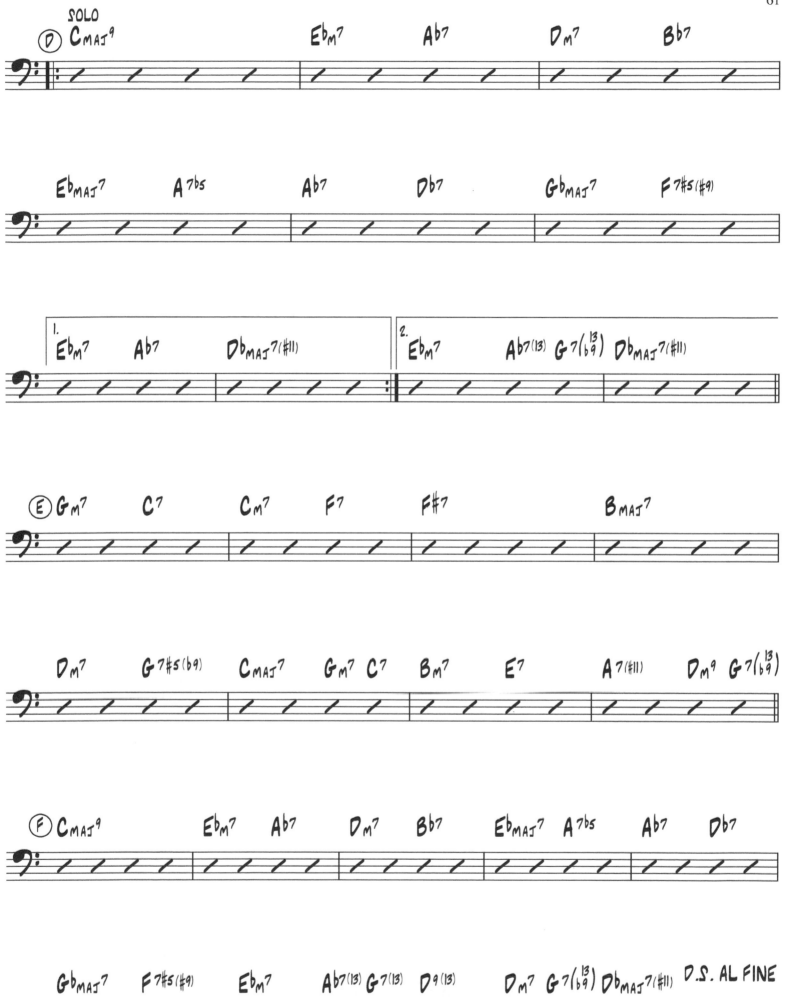

BRIGHT MISSISSIPPI

BY THELONIOUS MONK

Copyright © 1978 by Thelonious Music Corp.
This arrangement Copyright © 2010 by Thelonious Music Corp.
International Copyright Secured   All Rights Reserved

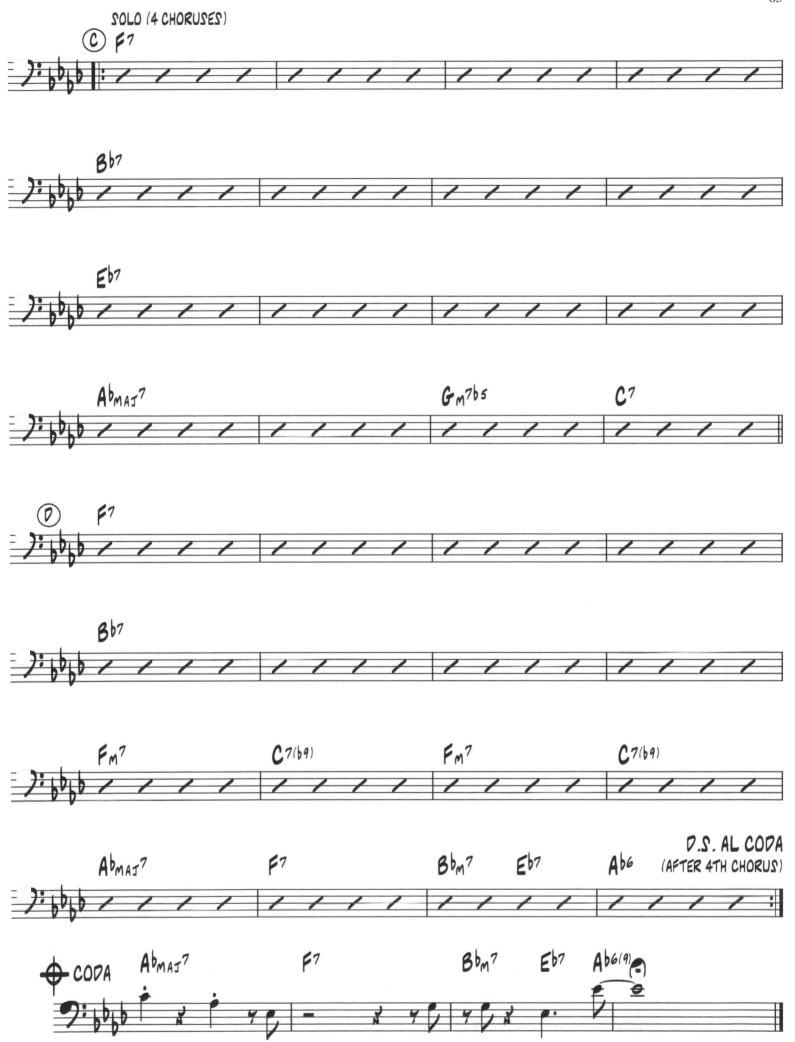

BEMSHA SWING

BY THELONIOUS MONK
AND DENZIL BEST

Copyright © 1952 (Renewed 1980) Second Floor Music
This arrangement Copyright © 2010 Second Floor Music
International Copyright Secured All Rights Reserved

BLUE MONK

♩: C VERSION

BY THELONIOUS MONK

SOLO (4 CHORUSES)

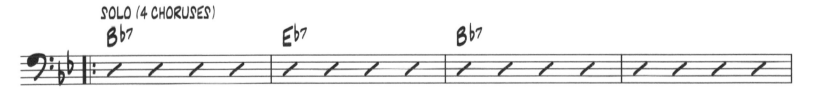

D.C. AL FINE
(AFTER 4TH CHORUS)

Copyright © 1962 (Renewed 1990) by Thelonious Music Corp.
This arrangement Copyright © 2010 by Thelonious Music Corp.
International Copyright Secured   All Rights Reserved

'ROUND MIDNIGHT

MUSIC BY THELONIOUS MONK AND COOTIE WILLIAMS
WORDS BY BERNIE HANIGHEN

Copyright © 1944 (Renewed 1971) by Thelonious Music Corp. and Warner Bros. Inc.
This arrangement Copyright © 2010 by Thelonious Music Corp. and Warner Bros. Inc.
International Copyright Secured   All Rights Reserved

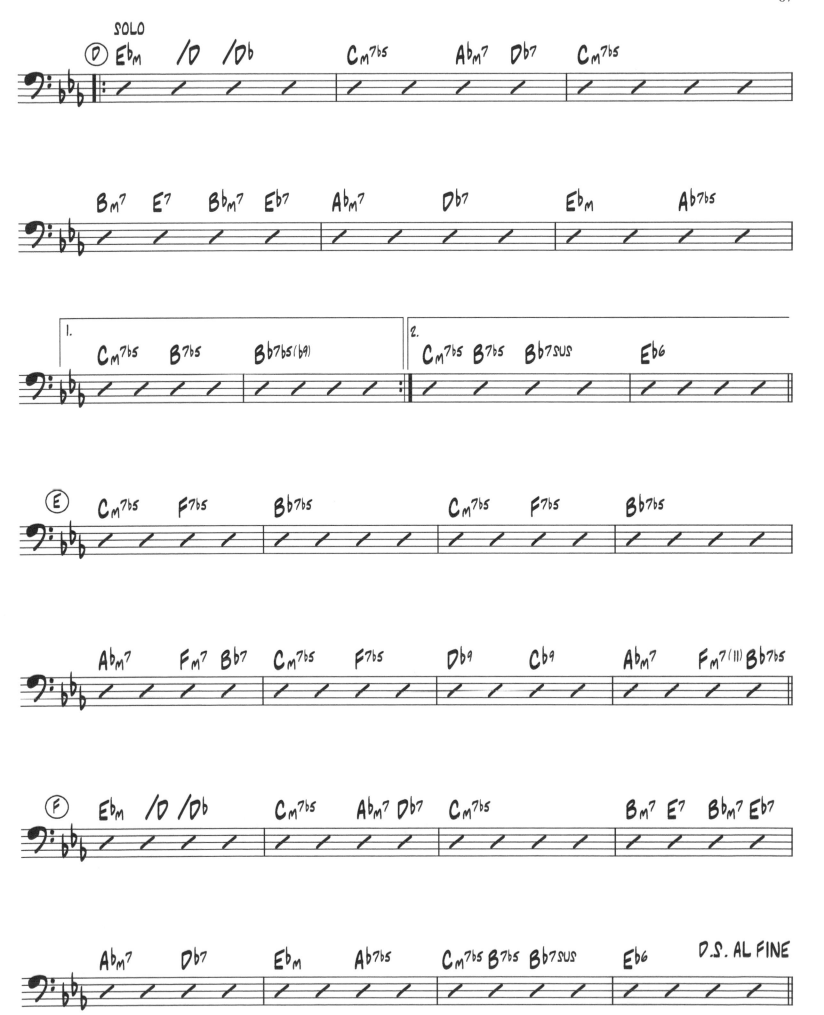

SHUFFLE BOIL

BY THELONIOUS MONK

Copyright © 1955 (Renewed 1984) by Thelonious Music Corp.
This arrangement Copyright © 2010 by Thelonious Music Corp.
International Copyright Secured   All Rights Reserved

UGLY BEAUTY

BY THELONIOUS MONK

* BOTH THE ♮5 AND ♭5 ARE VOICED IN THE HARMONY: THE ♮5 ABOVE THE ROOT, BELOW THE ♭5.

Copyright © 1978 by Thelonious Music Corp.
This arrangement Copyright © 2010 by Thelonious Music Corp.
International Copyright Secured   All Rights Reserved

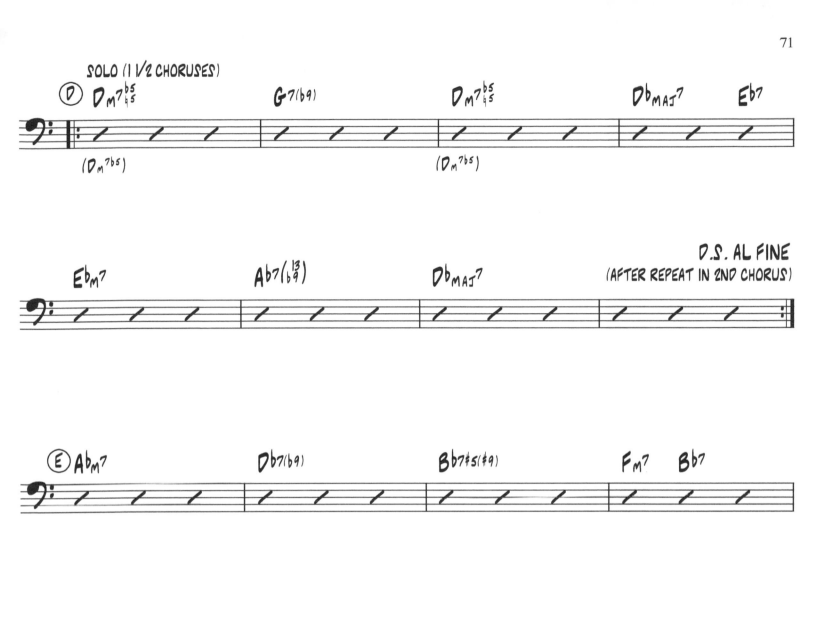

RHYTHM-A-NING

BY THELONIOUS MONK

𝄢 C VERSION

MEDIUM SWING

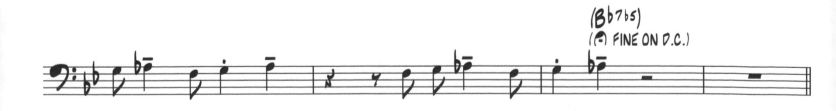

Copyright © 1958 (Renewed 1986) by Thelonious Music Corp.
This arrangement Copyright © 2010 by Thelonious Music Corp.
International Copyright Secured   All Rights Reserved

BYE-YA

BY THELONIOUS MONK

Copyright © 1962 (Renewed 1990) by Thelonious Music Corp.
This arrangement Copyright © 2010 by Thelonious Music Corp.
International Copyright Secured   All Rights Reserved

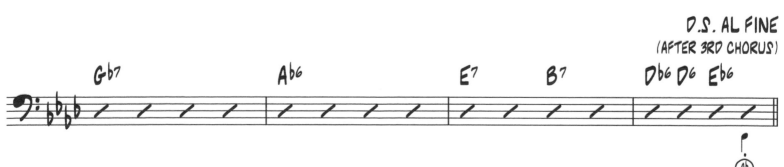

JAZZ PLAY-ALONG® SERIES

For use with all B-flat, E-flat, Bass Clef and C instruments, the **Jazz Play-Along Series** is the ultimate learning tool for all jazz musicians. With musician-friendly lead sheets, melody cues, and other split-track choices on the included audio, these first-of-a-kind packages help you master improvisation while playing some of the greatest tunes of all time.

FOR STUDY, each tune includes a split track with: melody cue with proper style and inflection • professional rhythm tracks • choruses for soloing • removable bass part • removable piano part.

FOR PERFORMANCE, each tune also has: an additional full stereo accompaniment track (no melody) • additional choruses for soloing.

To see full descriptions of all the books in the series, visit:

www.halleonard.com

The Best-Selling Jazz Book of All Time Is Now Legal!

The Real Books are the most popular jazz books of all time. Since the 1970s, musicians have trusted these volumes to get them through every gig, night after night. The problem is that the books were illegally produced and distributed, without any regard to copyright law, or royalties paid to the composers who created these musical masterpieces.

Hal Leonard is very proud to present the first legitimate and legal editions of these books ever produced. You won't even notice the difference, other than all the notorious errors being fixed: the covers and typeface look the same, the song lists are nearly identical, and the price for our edition is even cheaper than the originals!

Every conscientious musician will appreciate that these books are now produced accurately and ethically, benefitting the songwriters that we owe for some of the greatest tunes of all time!

VOLUME 1
00240221	C Edition	$49.99
00240224	Bb Edition	$49.99
00240225	Eb Edition	$49.99
00240226	Bass Clef Edition	$49.99
00286389	F Edition	$39.99
00240292	C Edition 6 x 9	$39.99
00240339	Bb Edition 6 x 9	$44.99
00147792	Bass Clef Edition 6 x 9	$39.99
00200984	Online Backing Tracks: Selections	$45.00
00110604	Book/USB Flash Drive Backing Tracks Pack	$85.00
00110599	USB Flash Drive Only	$50.00

VOLUME 2
00240222	C Edition	$49.99
00240227	Bb Edition	$49.99
00240228	Eb Edition	$49.99
00240229	Bass Clef Edition	$49.99
00240293	C Edition 6 x 9	$39.99
00125900	Bb Edition 6 x 9	$39.99
00125900	The Real Book – Mini Edition	$39.99
00204126	Backing Tracks on USB Flash Drive	$55.00
00204131	C Edition – USB Flash Drive Pack	$85.00

VOLUME 3
00240233	C Edition	$49.99
00240284	Bb Edition	$49.99
00240285	Eb Edition	$49.99
00240286	Bass Clef Edition	$49.99
00240338	C Edition 6 x 9	$39.99

VOLUME 4
00240296	C Edition	$49.99
00103348	Bb Edition	$49.99
00103349	Eb Edition	$49.99
00103350	Bass Clef Edition	$49.99

VOLUME 5
00240349	C Edition	$49.99
00175278	Bb Edition	$49.99
00175279	Eb Edition	$49.99

VOLUME 6
00240534	C Edition	$49.99
00223637	Eb Edition	$49.99

Also available:
00154230	The Real Bebop Book C Edition	$34.99
00295069	The Real Bebop Book Eb Edition	$34.99
00295068	The Real Bebop Book Bb Edition	$34.99
00240264	The Real Blues Book	$39.99
00310910	The Real Bluegrass Book	$39.99
00240223	The Real Broadway Book	$39.99
00240440	The Trane Book	$25.00
00125426	The Real Country Book	$45.00
00269721	The Real Miles Davis Book C Edition	$29.99
00269723	The Real Miles Davis Book Bb Edition	$29.99
00240355	The Real Dixieland Book C Edition	$39.99
00294853	The Real Dixieland Book Eb Edition	$39.99
00122335	The Real Dixieland Book Bb Edition	$39.99
00240235	The Duke Ellington Real Book	$29.99
00240268	The Real Jazz Solos Book	$44.99
00240348	The Real Latin Book C Edition	$39.99
00127107	The Real Latin Book Bb Edition	$39.99
00120809	The Pat Metheny Real Book C Edition	$34.99
00252119	The Pat Metheny Real Book Bb Edition	$29.99
00240358	The Charlie Parker Real Book C Edition	$25.00
00275997	The Charlie Parker Real Book Eb Edition	$25.00
00118324	The Real Pop Book C Edition – Vol. 1	$45.00
00295066	The Real Pop Book Bb Edition – Vol. 1	$39.99
00286451	The Real Pop Book C Edition – Vol. 2	$45.00
00240331	The Bud Powell Real Book	$25.00
00240437	The Real R&B Book C Edition	$45.00
00276590	The Real R&B Book Bb Edition	$45.00
00240313	The Real Rock Book	$39.99
00240323	The Real Rock Book – Vol. 2	$39.99
00240359	The Real Tab Book	$39.99
00240317	The Real Worship Book	$35.00

THE REAL CHRISTMAS BOOK
00240306	C Edition	$39.99
00240345	Bb Edition	$35.00
00240346	Eb Edition	$35.00
00240347	Bass Clef Edition	$35.00

THE REAL VOCAL BOOK
00240230	Volume 1 High Voice	$40.00
00240307	Volume 1 Low Voice	$40.00
00240231	Volume 2 High Voice	$39.99
00240308	Volume 2 Low Voice	$39.99
00240391	Volume 3 High Voice	$39.99
00240392	Volume 3 Low Voice	$39.99
00118318	Volume 4 High Voice	$39.99
00118319	Volume 4 Low Voice	$39.99

Complete song lists online at www.halleonard.com

Prices, content, and availability subject to change without notice.

0223
318

JAZZ INSTRUCTION & IMPROVISATION

BOOKS FOR ALL INSTRUMENTS FROM HAL LEONARD

500 JAZZ LICKS
by Brent Vaartstra

This book aims to assist you on your journey to play jazz fluently. These short phrases and ideas we call "licks" will help you understand how to navigate the common chords and chord progressions you will encounter. Adding this vocabulary to your arsenal will send you down the right path and improve your jazz playing, regardless of your instrument.
00142384 ....$16.99

1001 JAZZ LICKS
by Jack Shneidman
Cherry Lane Music

This book presents 1,001 melodic gems played over dozens of the most important chord progressions heard in jazz. This is the ideal book for beginners seeking a well-organized, easy-to-follow encyclopedia of jazz vocabulary, as well as professionals who want to take their knowledge of the jazz language to new heights.
02500133 ....$17.99

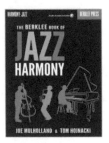

THE BERKLEE BOOK OF JAZZ HARMONY
by Joe Mulholland & Tom Hojnacki

Learn jazz harmony, as taught at Berklee College of Music. This text provides a strong foundation in harmonic principles, supporting further study in jazz composition, arranging, and improvisation. It covers basic chord types and their tensions, with practical demonstrations of how they are used in characteristic jazz contexts and an accompanying recording that lets you hear how they can be applied.
00113755 Book/Online Audio......................$34.99

BUILDING A JAZZ VOCABULARY
By Mike Steinel

A valuable resource for learning the basics of jazz from Mike Steinel of the University of North Texas. It covers: the basics of jazz • how to build effective solos • a comprehensive practice routine • and a jazz vocabulary of the masters.
00849911 ....$22.99

COMPREHENSIVE TECHNIQUE FOR JAZZ MUSICIANS
2ND EDITION
by Bert Ligon
Houston Publishing

An incredible presentation of the most practical exercises an aspiring jazz student could want. All are logically interwoven with fine "real world" examples from jazz to classical. This book is an essential anthology of technical, compositional, and theoretical exercises, with lots of musical examples.
00030455 ....$34.99

EAR TRAINING
by Keith Wyatt, Carl Schroeder and Joe Elliott
Musicians Institute Press

Covers: basic pitch matching • singing major and minor scales • identifying intervals • transcribing melodies and rhythm • identifying chords and progressions • seventh chords and the blues • modal interchange, chromaticism, modulation • and more.
00695198 Book/Online Audio......................$29.99

EXERCISES AND ETUDES FOR THE JAZZ INSTRUMENTALIST
by J.J. Johnson

Designed as study material and playable by any instrument, these pieces run the gamut of the jazz experience, featuring common and uncommon time signatures and keys, and styles from ballads to funk. They are progressively graded so that both beginners and professionals will be challenged by the demands of this wonderful music.
00842018 Bass Clef Edition $22.99
00842042 Treble Clef Edition $16.95

HOW TO PLAY FROM A REAL BOOK
by Robert Rawlins

Explore, understand, and perform the songs in real books with the techniques in this book. Learn how to analyze the form and harmonic structure, insert an introduction, interpret the melody, improvise on the chords, construct bass lines, voice the chords, add substitutions, and more. It addresses many aspects of solo and small band performance that can improve your own playing and your understanding of what others are doing around you.
00312097 ....$19.99

JAZZ DUETS
ETUDES FOR PHRASING AND ARTICULATION
by Richard Lowell
Berklee Press

With these 27 duets in jazz and jazz-influenced styles, you will learn how to improve your ear, sense of timing, phrasing, and your facility in bringing theoretical principles into musical expression. Covers: jazz staccato & legato • scales, modes & harmonies • phrasing within and between measures • swing feel • and more.
00302151 ....$14.99

JAZZ THEORY & WORKBOOK
by Lilian Dericq & Étienne Guéreau

Designed for all instrumentalists, this book teaches how jazz standards are constructed. It is also a great resource for arrangers and composers seeking new writing tools. While some of the musical examples are pianistic, this book is not exclusively for keyboard players.
00159022 ....$19.99

JAZZ THEORY RESOURCES
by Bert Ligon
Houston Publishing, Inc.

This is a jazz theory text in two volumes. **Volume 1 includes:** review of basic theory • rhythm in jazz performance • triadic generalization • diatonic harmonic progressions and analysis • substitutions and turnarounds • and more. **Volume 2 includes:** modes and modal frameworks • quartal harmony • extended tertian structures and triadic superimposition • pentatonic applications • coloring "outside" the lines and beyond • and more.
00030458 Volume 1 ....$39.99
00030459 Volume 2 ....$32.99

JAZZOLOGY
THE ENCYCLOPEDIA OF JAZZ THEORY FOR ALL MUSICIANS
by Robert Rawlins and Nor Eddine Bahha

This comprehensive resource covers a variety of jazz topics, for beginners and pros of any instrument. The book serves as an encyclopedia for reference, a thorough methodology for the student, and a workbook for the classroom.
00311167 ....$24.99

MODALOGY
SCALES, MODES & CHORDS: THE PRIMORDIAL BUILDING BLOCKS OF MUSIC
by Jeff Brent with Schell Barkley

Primarily a music theory reference, this book presents a unique perspective on the origins, interlocking aspects, and usage of the most common scales and modes in occidental music. Anyone wishing to seriously explore the realms of scales, modes, and their real-world functions will find the most important issues dealt with in meticulous detail within these pages.
00312274 ....$24.99

THE SOURCE
THE DICTIONARY OF CONTEMPORARY AND TRADITIONAL SCALES
by Steve Barta

This book serves as an informative guide for people who are looking for good, solid information regarding scales, chords, and how they work together. It provides right and left hand fingerings for scales, chords, and complete inversions. Includes over 20 different scales, each written in all 12 keys.
00240885 ....$21.99

www.halleonard.com

Prices, contents & availability subject to change without notice.

0523
068

ARTIST TRANSCRIPTIONS®

Artist Transcriptions are authentic, note-for-note transcriptions of today's hottest artists in jazz, pop and rock. These outstanding, accurate arrangements are in an easy-to-read format which includes all essential lines. **Artist Transcriptions** can be used to perform, sequence or for reference.

FLUTE

00672379	Eric Dolphy Collection	$19.95
00672582	The Very Best of James Galway	$19.99
00672372	James Moody Collection – Sax and Flute	$19.95

GUITAR & BASS

00660113	Guitar Style of George Benson	$19.99
00672573	Ray Brown – Legendary Jazz Bassist	$22.99
00672331	Ron Carter Collection	$24.99
00660115	Al Di Meola – Friday Night in San Francisco	$24.99
00125617	Best of Herb Ellis	$19.99
00699306	Jim Hall – Exploring Jazz Guitar	$19.99
00672353	The Joe Pass Collection	$22.99
00673216	John Patitucci	$22.99
00672374	Johnny Smith – Guitar Solos	$24.99

PIANO & KEYBOARD

00672487	Monty Alexander Plays Standards	$19.95
00672520	Count Basie Collection	$19.95
00192307	Bebop Piano Legends	$19.99
00113680	Blues Piano Legends	$22.99
00672526	The Bill Charlap Collection	$19.99
00278003	A Charlie Brown Christmas	$19.99
00672300	Chick Corea – Paint the World	$19.99
00146105	Bill Evans – Alone	$21.99
00672548	The Mastery of Bill Evans	$16.99
00672365	Bill Evans – Play Standards	$22.99
00121885	Bill Evans – Time Remembered	$22.99
00672510	Bill Evans Trio Vol. 1: 1959-1961	$29.99
00672511	Bill Evans Trio Vol. 2: 1962-1965	$27.99
00672512	Bill Evans Trio Vol. 3: 1968-1974	$29.99
00672513	Bill Evans Trio Vol. 4: 1979-1980	$24.95
00193332	Erroll Garner – Concert by the Sea	$22.99
00672486	Vince Guaraldi Collection	$19.99
00289644	The Definitive Vince Guaraldi	$39.99
00672419	Herbie Hancock Collection	$24.99
00672438	Hampton Hawes Collection	$19.95
00672322	Ahmad Jamal Collection	$27.99
00255671	Jazz Piano Masterpieces	$22.99
00124367	Jazz Piano Masters Play Rodgers & Hammerstein	$19.99
00672564	Best of Jeff Lorber	$19.99
00672476	Brad Mehldau Collection	$24.99

00672388	Best of Thelonious Monk	$24.99
00672389	Thelonious Monk Collection	$24.99
00672390	Thelonious Monk Plays Jazz Standards – Volume 1	$24.99
00672391	Thelonious Monk Plays Jazz Standards – Volume 2	$24.99
00264094	Oscar Peterson – Night Train	$22.99
00672544	Oscar Peterson – Originals	$17.99
00672531	Oscar Peterson – Plays Duke Ellington	$27.99
00672563	Oscar Peterson – A Royal Wedding Suite	$19.99
00672569	Oscar Peterson – Tracks	$19.99
00672533	Oscar Peterson – Trios	$39.99
00672534	Very Best of Oscar Peterson	$29.99
00672371	Bud Powell Classics	$22.99
00672376	Bud Powell Collection	$24.99
00672507	Gonzalo Rubalcaba Collection	$19.95
00672316	Art Tatum Collection	$27.99
00672355	Art Tatum Solo Book	$22.99
00672357	The Billy Taylor Collection	$24.95
00673215	McCoy Tyner	$22.99
00672321	Cedar Walton Collection	$19.95
00672519	Kenny Werner Collection	$19.95

SAXOPHONE

00672566	The Mindi Abair Collection	$14.99
00673244	Julian "Cannonball" Adderley Collection	$22.99
00673237	Michael Brecker	$24.99
00672429	Michael Brecker Collection	$24.99
00672529	John Coltrane – Giant Steps	$22.99
00672494	John Coltrane – A Love Supreme	$17.99
00672493	John Coltrane Plays "Coltrane Changes"	$19.95
00672453	John Coltrane Plays Standards	$25.99
00673233	John Coltrane Solos	$29.99
00672328	Paul Desmond Collection	$22.99
00672530	Kenny Garrett Collection	$24.99
00699375	Stan Getz	$24.99
00672377	Stan Getz – Bossa Novas	$24.99
00673254	Great Tenor Sax Solos	$22.99
00672523	Coleman Hawkins Collection	$24.99
00673239	Best of Kenny G	$22.99
00673229	Kenny G – Breathless	$19.99
00672462	Kenny G – Classics in the Key of G	$26.99

00672485	Kenny G – Faith: A Holiday Album	$17.99
00672373	Kenny G – The Moment	$22.99
00672498	Jackie McLean Collection	$19.95
00672372	James Moody Collection – Sax and Flute	$19.95
00672539	Gerry Mulligan Collection	$24.99
00102751	Sonny Rollins, Art Blakey & Kenny Drew with the Modern Jazz Quartet	$17.99
00675000	David Sanborn Collection	$19.99
00672491	The New Best of Wayne Shorter	$24.99
00672550	The Sonny Stitt Collection	$19.95
00672524	Lester Young Collection	$22.99

TROMBONE

00672332	J.J. Johnson Collection	$24.99
00672489	Steve Turré Collection	$19.99

TRUMPET

00672557	Herb Alpert Collection	$19.99
00672480	Louis Armstrong Collection	$22.99
00672481	Louis Armstrong Plays Standards	$22.99
00672435	Chet Baker Collection	$24.99
00672556	Best of Chris Botti	$21.99
00672448	Miles Davis – Originals, Vol. 1	$19.99
00672451	Miles Davis – Originals, Vol. 2	$19.95
00672449	Miles Davis – Standards, Vol. 2	$19.95
00672479	Dizzy Gillespie Collection	$19.95
00673214	Freddie Hubbard	$19.99
00672506	Chuck Mangione Collection	$22.99

HAL•LEONARD®

Visit our web site for songlists or to order online from your favorite music retailer at
www.halleonard.com

Prices, content, and availability subject to change without notice.